First World War
and Army of Occupation
War Diary
France, Belgium and Germany

51 DIVISION
154 Infantry Brigade,
Brigade Trench Mortar Battery
3 September 1916 - 31 December 1916

WO95/2888/4

The Naval & Military Press Ltd
www.nmarchive.com
Published in association with The National Archives

Published by

The Naval & Military Press Ltd

Unit 10 Ridgewood Industrial Park,

Uckfield, East Sussex,

TN22 5QE England

Tel: +44 (0) 1825 749494

www.naval-military-press.com

www.nmarchive.com

This diary has been reprinted in facsimile from the original. Any imperfections are inevitably reproduced and the quality may fall short of modern type and cartographic standards.

© **Crown Copyright**
Images reproduced by permission of The National Archives, London, England, 2015.

Contents

Document type	Place/Title	Date From	Date To
Heading	WO95/2888/3 154 Brigade Trench Mortar Battery		
Heading	51 Div 154 Bde 154 Trench Mortar Bty 1916 Sep-1916 Dec		
War Diary	Albert		
War Diary	Authville	03/09/1916	03/09/1916
War Diary	Albert	16/09/1916	16/09/1916
War Diary	Henencourt	18/09/1916	20/09/1916
War Diary	Authville	21/09/1916	21/09/1916
War Diary	Aveluy	30/09/1916	12/10/1916
War Diary	Authville	15/10/1916	15/10/1916
War Diary	Aveluy	23/10/1916	23/10/1916
War Diary	Authville	26/10/1916	27/10/1916
War Diary	Aveluy	09/11/1916	10/11/1916
War Diary	Authville	14/11/1916	14/11/1916
War Diary	Aveluy	17/11/1916	17/11/1916
War Diary	Henencourt	27/11/1916	27/11/1916
War Diary	Lavieville	30/11/1916	23/12/1916
War Diary	Authville	24/12/1916	31/12/1916

WO95/2888/3

154 Brigade Trench Mortar Battery

51 DIV
154 Bde

154 TRENCH
MORTAR BTY

1916 SEP – 1916 DEC

Army Form C. 2118.

WAR DIARY
or
INTELLIGENCE SUMMARY.
(Erase heading not required.)

Instructions regarding War Diaries and Intelligence Summaries are contained in F. S. Regs., Part II. and the Staff Manual respectively. Title pages will be prepared in manuscript.

Place	Date	Hour	Summary of Events and Information	Remarks and references to Appendices
ALBERT			During this period it was possible to obtain large fatigue parties to carry ammunition into the trenches, as many as 75 men at a time being placed at our disposal in one am. Generally the ammunition supply was ample and the quality good.	Watermark on title page regarding this point.
AUTHUILLE	Sept 3rd		2nd Lt. HARTER was ordered to take 2 guns into E. Sector, to the road Indian Cavalry Division Hdqrs, and marched in that day. Ammunition became very scarce and of various power grades, specially as regards fuses and T tubes. There was at first have difficulty about returning the batteries, as but had no carts and this occurred again when the 1st Indian Cavalry Division came up and again when they handed to the 153rd Inf. Bde.

The enemy relied on light trench mortars and the "Minnen" or "old drums". These had to be reported to us at LA BOISSELLE, but they were steadily increasing in numbers and effect at AUTHUILLE during September, as many as six being fired at once towards the end of that month which greatly worried them and our effect. | From [illegible]... on 16 September... heavy types... etc. etc. further used... to be made with regard not to use (?) in the latter as at LA BOISSELLE. |

2353 Wt. W2514/1454 700,000 5/15 D. D. & L. A.D.S.S./Forms/C. 2118.

WAR DIARY
or
INTELLIGENCE SUMMARY.

(Erase heading not required.)

Place	Date	Hour	Summary of Events and Information	Remarks and references to Appendices
ALBERT	Sept 17th		Sgt. HINDSON, R.G.A., was sent home and Sgt. BRERETON, R.F.A., sent to the Battery in his place.	Note records on letter from regarding the sheet
HENENCOURT	Sept 18th		Lt. WATERHOUSE and his half Battery withdrew from action for replacement at HENENCOURT.	
	Sept 20th		Lt. HARPER submitted a request to be transferred to a field battery.	
AUTHUILLE	Sept 21st		Lt. WATERHOUSE and his half battery rejoined Lt. HARPER and the half battery at AUTHUILLE. Three 95mm French Mortars and 7 men to work them were attached to us for the remainder of our duty at AUTHUILLE.	
AVELUY	Sept 30th		The battery joined its own Bde., the 150th, at AVELUY. Some days were spent in reconnoitering and digging emplacements in F₂ sector.	
"	Oct 17th		The battery put four guns into action in F₂.	
AUTHUILLE	Oct 15th-17th		Lt. HARPER ordered to take 2 guns and 10 men to AUTHUILLE and report to Major WAKLEY, O.C. 88th Trench Battery there. Control action was arranged for and taken with the 91st and 81st French Batteries.	

Army Form C. 2118.

WAR DIARY
or
INTELLIGENCE SUMMARY.
(Erase heading not required.)

Instructions regarding War Diaries and Intelligence Summaries are contained in F.S. Regs., Part II. and the Staff Manual respectively. Title pages will be prepared in manuscript.

Place	Date	Hour	Summary of Events and Information	Remarks and references to Appendices
AVELUY	Sept. 23rd		2nd Lt. P. CLARKE, 3rd Wilts, joined the Battery, Lt WATERHOUSE being recalled to his battalion. Lt WATERHOUSE submitted an application to return command, and Lt. HARPER took over command of the battery.	
AUTHUILLE	Oct. 20th		Lt HARPER appeared to have the battery enrolled and working in only six days at a time and rejected AVELUY on the better billets. Reasons given included difficulty of reaching and returning units of relative and extra trouble involved in cooking and rationing from two centres. Permission given to regard AVELUY as Hqrs. for the Wilts battery, and a few days later we were permitted to withdraw our guns from	
"	Oct. 27th		G sector and place them all in F. During this period Lt HARPER reported the need of electric flash lamps for night work, and of a bright and too linnen in order to keep papers in book with the work of the battery.	
AVELUY	Nov. 9th		On the order of the Brigadier Commanding issued 2/Lt Blake in AVELUY at that time, the battery prepared a scheme in conjunction with the 98th Trench Battery for their interoperation in the sector.	
"	Nov. 11th		The two batteries submitted an alteration in their original scheme, again at the instance of the Brigade. The essential point was to maintain	

2353 Wt. W2544/1454 700,000 5/15 D. D. & L. A.D.S.S./Forms/C. 2118.

WAR DIARY
or
INTELLIGENCE SUMMARY.
(Erase heading not required.)

Army Form C. 2118.

Place	Date	Hour	Summary of Events and Information	Remarks and references to Appendices
AUTHUILLE	Nov. 14th		the closest possible touch between the artillery and Infantry commanders, and it was suggested that a Trench Battery Officer should be stationed at H.Qrs. of the left Battalion for this purpose, and that the guns must all be linked up to him and the observation posts by Telephone. Telephones were required for the whole scheme.	Not much to take place regarding this place
AVELUY HENENCOURT	Nov. 17th		Captain BATESON, R.G.A. met all the Trench Battery officers of the division at AUTHUILLE and discussed our work. Lt. HARPER recommended that fuses be carried distributed up to the Guns.	
	Nov. 27th		The firing being done very irregular owing to the use of L.S. tubes and adapters (there were also cuts use at the end of October) and the tubes dropping about 50% short, the next 7 N.M. school of instruction was withdrawn to HENENCOURT till new supplies of ammunition could be issued. The L.S. tubes were thats afterwards withdrawn and firing with the old type of fuse forbidden.	
LAVIEVILLE	Nov. 30th		The battery was moved to LAVIEVILLE to make room for the Scottish Rifles and Loyal N. Lancs.	

WAR DIARY
or
INTELLIGENCE SUMMARY.
(Erase heading not required.)

Army Form C. 2118.

Place	Date	Hour	Summary of Events and Information	Remarks and references to Appendices
LAVIEVILLE	Dec 4th		Lt HARPER proceeded to England on leave.	Note remarks on last page regarding casualties this week.
	Dec 11th		Sgt. BRERETON proceeded to exchange with Sgt. ATKINS, R.G.A. from the 92nd Trench Battery.	
	Dec 13th		Lt HARPER returned to duty. A second application to be transferred to full battery, on the grounds that he had been gazetted to the 18 pounder and had only a few days training with Trench Mortars was refused on the grounds that there was a shortage of R.A. Officers and he could not be replaced.	
	Dec 18th		The new batteries were mortars were returned to us to be looked after, the Heavy M/C Workshop, BEAUVAL, Mons had been sufficiently recovered. On 7 gun sets acting with the 159th Inf. Bde. our 6 came across the battery but not 7 gun sets acting with the 159th Inf. Bde. coming to heavy no fuses for its mortars. The 98th Trench Battery returned practice. We continued with gun drill, lectures, and instruction instead of making wide emplacements as when we first came to LAVIEVILLE.	
	Dec 20th 21st		Warned by Bde. Major 159th Inf. Bde. to go into C. sector as soon as founded with ammunition. To have 2 wagons for transport. To work under Captn RALSTON, machine gun officer of the Bde. Telephones to be furnished.	

WAR DIARY or INTELLIGENCE SUMMARY

Army Form C. 2118.

Place	Date	Hour	Summary of Events and Information	Remarks and references to Appendices
LAVIEVILLE	22 Dec.		Lt. HARPER attended Divisional HQrs. to represent the Battery at a Conference, where full details were requested and given concerning the ammunition used by 15" Trench Mortars. Two G.S. waggons & one 3 ton motor van forwarded for transporting the battery when ordered.	
"	23rd Dec.	1 a.m.	Telegram received 15th Infy. Bde. to move Battery to MARTINSART. & G.S. waggons wanted before 9 am. Loaded up, but there were very few and plenty of all kinds being in billets under orders from the Bde. Machine Gun Officer & B.D.E. MAJOR just the Battery. B.M.G.O. ordered us to report at this and moved us in to Authuille. B.M.G.O. ordered us to report at this guns vilely and to retaliate under fire and any bit. Lt. HARPER pointed out that this plan was contrary to instructions from First Div. and could not accept it on his own authority. B.M.G.O. took full responsibility for this order and we therefore proceeded to engage. Recommenced and preformed firstams. 88th Trench Battery has 2 guns here. Ditto. MkII light ammunition intended for did not come, but MkI instead. Opened fire from G3 and G2. Fuses not very good but their timing inaccurate and four air bursts resulted. 8 light bursts fired.	
AUTHUILLE	24th			
"	25th			
"	26th		Motor relations in fr	

WAR DIARY
or
INTELLIGENCE SUMMARY

Army Form C. 2118.

Place	Date	Hour	Summary of Events and Information	Remarks and references to Appendices
AUTHUILE	27th		Fired 6 rounds from G.3. Morphid retaliation. Fired 7 rounds from G.1. and made a junction in left of G.1. Requested B.M.G.O. to assist us in recovering 2 Howitzers and 3 Howitzer barrels. Light Ordnance Workshops Returnd, when they have been refurring. Also that he could arrange to send me 1 no 10th bolts & Ordnance for immediate + immediate later. Received orders for a shoot in [?] with artillery for 2.30 P.M.	
"	28th		Borrowed a gun from 98th Trench Battery at Authuille and kept it up to 9 Grunner. Shot on left 7 G.1. Left G.3 in charge 7 Cpl McDowell who was wounded – the head 7 shrapnel after firing 1? rounds. He returned, but bed purified and Leary Shrapnel prevented him returning and he was ordered into shelter by my Officer on duty. He reports his gun was not 7 action by anything his injury which was slight, and later removed fire trees as ordered before his wound was dressed, dressed by Stretcher bearers by his Officer. G.3 & bomb G.1 fired 10 Mk II heavy and 10 Mk I light bombs, there being great difficulty with fuel trays and shifting beds. A large and	

WAR DIARY
or
INTELLIGENCE SUMMARY.

(Erase heading not required.)

Army Form C. 2118.

Place	Date	Hour	Summary of Events and Information	Remarks and references to Appendices
AUTHUILLE	29th		Guns in enemy's rep trench were firing into the air 5 me I on Mk II bomb. There were 2 bombs with the Mk I and I with the Mk II here. No retaliation. In 6, we got off 17 rounds, 8 being of Mk I heavy, one of Mk I lighter and one Mk II. One bd perfect one a little shorter, one fell here. We had my three filmers not in clipped. With a accurate gun system we could have got better results. Lt. HARPER transferred higher up asked the off Captain 158th 2/, Bde. for assistance to recover the premises and trees mentioned over at RIBEMONT. Bohs re-set.	
"	30th		See two trees on right of road in G3 to fire in air mode in front of "Hammerhead". Plan to fire 2 rounds at 6 and 2 at 6.5 P.M. with artillery and 2" mortar support, to drive enemy Inhbtr from much road. Fired one off at 6 P.M. and 2 at 6.5 P.M. very to 3 minpis. Bombs burst well, Mk I. 3s &s.	
"	31st		Fired 8 light bombs from 6 & 8 Mk I. heavy bombs from Inversary Jct and 10 from Burial Trench on G, Rhid.	

www.ingramcontent.com/pod-product-compliance
Lightning Source LLC
Chambersburg PA
CBHW081513160426
43193CB00014B/2675